faith and identity

Margaret Tran

BookLeaf Publishing

India | USA | UK

Presentation by *BookLeaf Publishing*

Web: www.bookleafpub.com

E-mail: info@bookleafpub.com

ISBN: 9789357211765

First edition 2023

DEDICATION

I dedicate this little book to my birth mother I never met, my beloved adoptive mother who raised me with her unconditional love. I also want to dedicate to my husband who went through hardship together, my three newly found sisters, and last but not least, my beautiful children. This one is for you, from me, your loving daughter, wife, mom, and baby sister.

ACKNOWLEDGEMENT

Writing a poem book is always exciting and fun. What I share with you in the pages that follow comes from over thirty-five years of meeting, learning from and being mentored by some amazing people.

In my life, I was shunned, bullied, molested, raped, but I did not lose my faith and self-worth. I have been blessed by my best friend, TOAnh, who helped me finding my identity. I am grateful to all of my friends and family who not only know who I can be and what I am capable of, but who, more importantly, expect more of me than I do of myself. This has made me a better person.

These people have given me the strength, courage and support to explore and take on challenges on my road to success. None of these are more important than my best friends, husband, and many more whose absolute love, trust, and support me over the years to achieve my dreams, goals and become who I am.

PREFACE

I was the only child growing with my adoptive mother in a communist regime. Growing up I was lonely, bullied and shunned by my own people. I felt ashamed, worthless, and angry. I became timid and afraid to speak up. Becoming a wife and mother changed my perspective of life. I wanted to know my root by searching for my biological parents.

After I lost my adoptive mother in 2012, I fell into a deep depression. An inner healing journey helped me recover so that I could be more present for my family. That growth process also inspired me to become a writer. I realized I could help others with my life story to guide others seeking to regain a sense of purpose and happiness.

As an avid reader, I recognized that there weren't many poems out there like mine. This book is for everyone who's struggling to find their own identity, faith, self-worth and place in the world. In my book, you'll find poems or stories and mementos that I hope will touch your heart.

Before writing this book, I published The
ACTIONS. It offers a summary and practical
guide to help you work through the seven steps
as defined by the 7 steps ACTIONS
Methodology.

Thank you to my friends and family for
supporting me throughout the most challenging
times.

i will rise

i was lost in life
didn't know what to do
how do i start my day
what does my heart desire
didn't know where i belong
where do i go from here
what mask to place on today
didn't know how to change
can someone help me
how do i turn around

i was lost in life
just trying to get by
i looked in the mirror
my eyes spoke to me
i don't want to be this
camouflage myself
a reason to survive
i will fight for it
after falling once and twice
i will rise myself

after every fall
i will rise myself
over the water and above them all
i rise like the sun

shining and brightly
i rise like a tree
standing strong and tall
nothing can hold me down
again and again
i will rise and rise

faith

faith
is a peculiar feeling
it's an expression of hope
life
would fail if there's no faith
which
is hard to express and identify

faith
is important as air
when things feel impossible
faith
nourishes our heart and soul
life
isn't always easy
we
all go through storms

faith
speaks the language of the heart
through the trials and tribulations
faith
helps to get us through,
even when things were tough
faith

inspired us never to give up

faith
impacts our lives
as we go about our day
faith
is a complete trust
incorporate faith into your life
simply
be grateful with joy

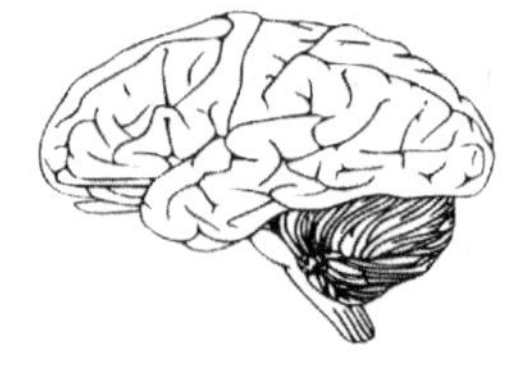

a mother who gave birth to me

the greatest gift
i was given from
was a mother who gave birth to me
due to the
unknown situation
you gave
me away
i have no choice
where to be
born into
but i do not hate or
regret being borne

i yearned for
one day
i can find you
so that
i can give you
a big hug
and cooed to you that
i love you
i want to tell you
all of my heartaches
all of my experiences as

i was growing up
and how others
bullied me

kids
at school blocked
my road
every day
neighbors
teased me with songs
and made fun of me
i was afraid
to go out
but i was still
a child
i still asked
i was forbidden
to go out
to play

at eleven
i came to
america
with hope and opportunities
here people
treated me like
a human
no disparage
no harassed

i played
with them like
normal children
without racist
america
is my second
home
with so much
love

i wish
you can experience
all this
with me
i no longer
feel afraid
no longer
have to hide
i feel happy
i feel free

the greatest gift
i was given from
was a mother who
gave birth
to me
i yearned for
one day
i can find you

so that
i can give you
a big hug
and cooed
to you that
i love you!

a mother who gave me life

a mother who gave me life
a life not yet to be enjoyed
turned around and gave me away
was it for love or for hate
did you ever look back
have you ever searched for me
all the questions boil in my mind

a mother who gave me life
no matter what you've done
i always appreciated you
appreciated the life you gave me
grateful that you gave me away
don't know how life would be with you
i know how my life would be without you.

a mother who gave me life
i missed you and truly loved you
never hate or disrespect
i wished one day i can find you
to ask you what had happened
i wished one day i can find you.

so i can hold you in my arms
i can call you my mother

i wished i can find you one day
i can repay my debt to you.

a mother who gave me life
do you ever wonder how i look like
i do wonder how you look like
how would i react if i find you
what would you say when you look at me

truth revealed

when i was eleven
mom and i
went to the interview
to go to
america
the interviewer said
my dear girl
you will go to america
by yourself
what would
a little girl
think
i was scared!
as i was
looking around
and thinking
in my head,
mom,
where are you?
as i wept
i replied
i will stay
with my mom
even if
i starve to death

my mom then
entered into
the room
without any knowledge
of what's going on
her arms
were wide open
wrapping me
in her arms
she
who never showed
her emotions
for the
first time said
i love you
the interviewer
said
that's the true unconditional love
from a mother
to a daughter
even
it's not her own
for the first time
i found out
i was adopted
i didn't care
all i know
that
i am loved

forgive

i forgive you
the man
i called
dad
the man
mom called
my lover
i forgive you
dad
a father figure
i've been yearning for
i thought
you
loved mom
with your betrayal
you
no longer
deserved her
i thought
you
cared for
me
such a pedophile
you have
done

me wrong
once you're gone
i can have
my mother back
i truly do
forgive you.

identity

when i was
young
i was ashamed
of how i looked
did not
understand why
i was
bullied
by other kids
when i was
young,
it was hard to
understand why
kids calling me
names
i hated
my life for not
being able
to speak up
when i was
young
it was hard to
understand
why i felt
worthless

i became a
shy
timid girl

everyday
was the same
since
at the young
age
in the mirror
i looked
i was ashamed of
my identity

"who am i?"
i asked
a silence
in the air,
no one
i can ask,
why
life so
unfair

it's okay
my sweetheart
"i am always
here for you,"
my mother said

they're all just
jealous
of your
beautiful heart

life is full of trials
and conflicts
it can
derail our moral hearts
betrayals
and rejections
as parts of our
life lessons

learn to respond
with love
selflessness
we grow
our hearts
so that
we can bring
joy into life

things changed when
i moved away
as i grew
older
a best friend
helped me see

not
everyone is bad

many people are
out there
waiting to be
my friends
they can help me
stand
firm
strong
and thriving

my
shell
had peeled off
i did well in school
made many
new friends
my feelings of
worthlessness
disappeared

i felt more
confident
my
identity
became clear
i am

patient
loving
kind
who deserved
to show up fully
in the world

i felt more
confident
i changed from
the shy
to appreciate
and kind
the core of
my identity
became clear

take on the world

graduation was a day
to mark a tremendous accomplishment
yet
a day to disappoint

i could not have come
to this day
without a lot of
hard work
yet
hard work went to waste

graduation was a moment to savor
the mind panics as
i mounted the stage of
my coming age
what to be
what to do

while everyone was celebrating
i was
devastated
over the
misunderstanding
the unknown reason

No one
came to my graduation

as the man
who i called
dad
slapped me
by surprised
i was broken down and bruised
i knew nothing but the pain

this one word could be
the segue
for my thought
process
i can't begin to tell you how much
HATE
i had
feeling so alone
so lost

suffering
day after day
there's no reason
to stay
couldn't find a way out
i grew tired of being in this drought

feeling

as if i would never be cared for
not being able to
spread
my wings
and soar

memories
that feel as if
they occurred
yesterday
turn to
flashes of moments
that seems
to fade away

before i knew
the light
i had my fair share
of darkness, too
where my world
fell into a
hopelessness
i didn't know
how to get through

i may not
have life figured out
but trust me
that's okay

life is full of
challenges
there may have been
days
when i felt that
i could not continue
yet, i did

unknown destination
no matter
where life leads
no matter
what you do
life is
what you make
do follow your plan

mistakes
were to be made
i moved on and
got back
on my two feet alone

before i was
who i am now
i was someone
i didn't want to be
i was lost
battered

defeated
before I knew
how to be me

sometimes things
in life
are bad
finding good
in the bad
giving thanks
despite negative

what's lost in life
just trying to get by
wishing
hoping
wondering
waiting
for the time that
i can fly

find my passion
find my drive
find something
that makes you fight
I am the driver
of my destiny
the captain
of my ship

journey
full of ups and downs
experience
gained each day
direction
is always forward and backwards
yet remains the same

discover
your authentic self
enhance
each quality given
develop
talents you were blessed

transform
your heart into gold
i have come so far
it's the time
for me to shine
now go on
take on the world

honoring you, your life

honoring your life
on your memorial day
you're gone and took
the wind with sunshine
ten years, with heartaches
i missed you
leaving me with all the
pain and regrets
but your beautiful image is
always with me

at your altar
i light the heart incense
heartfelt
sending you with
all of my love
i always remember
the merits of you
water flowing in the river
like a mother's love
with gratitude to remember
your nurture

i wish you're still here
with me now

so i can repay my
indebtedness to you
with your advice
i engraved in my heart
love all of the people
you have loved
i fulfilled my promise
mother
mother's love
mother's divine callings

as i pray
you're shining down on me
to the young people,
love mom
love dad
with filial
peace
family is forever joyful

god's lead

when we first met
my heart was numb
you teased me, dear
the time i was lost
you came and take
my hardships away
the day we met
i had no clue
so many things
pushed me to you
certain time in my life
you were my strengths
my shining armor
but i didn't care

another time in my life
you're my lifesaver
my strong protector
but i didn't appreciate
now is the time to reflect
upon my heart
nothing can compare
so to you these words
i've written from my heart
what was getting ready to happen

i'm following god's lead,
an important link to grow
even on our troubled days
not sure about the path we chose
on any given day
for better or for worst
i've always longing
a happy ending

life was always unexpected
with many ups and downs
for all the today and tomorrow
with laugh, cry, and remember
we worked things out right
there were many times in our path
you have cheated on me
oh how my heart ached
i chose a different path
to forgive and forget
was it a wise choice
many people have asked me
am i crazy to do this
as i said what matters is
that he still holds my heart.

there was such a big space between us
but we came through it
although it always seemed to mean
it was well worth it

i have the greatest respect
i had a wonderful time
we've shared the blessings
bestow
you have changed my life
and everything you did
some i take for granted
but nothing can be stronger
than my love for you

you give me all i ever need
you give me so much more
you bring me much delight
nothing can come between us
especially love from inside
your heart i fondly hold
with treasures you shower me
all the memories through
these years
i will always cherish them
i need to tell you a secret
i always forget to tell you that
our journey trials and conflict
can derail our relationships
for all of my beliefs and faith
love will conquer all

like mom used to say
always look at people

at their best
turn our hurt
betrayals
into understanding forgiveness
while in this world
we'll have
our smiles
our frowns
when our love is strong
all our frowns
seem to drown

we're just following god's lead
for honesty shines bright
we're not taking any chances
we're sincerely counting the blessings
knowing the path
i choose
in my life
i am at
ease
free
for all god's world to see

prayers had answered

since the time i understood
everyday is like a century
never a moment i gave up hope
forty seven years have come and gone
today is the day to reflect

life is just a trial
we have ups and downs
what we have was bliss
with sorrow and grief

i grew up alone
no siblings or friends
i was a bullied child
lived in fear for years

being molested cut me deep
a horrible feeling deep inside
i'm not always the best
putting on a smiling mask
life gets harder everyday
never a moment i gave up hope

faith is at its core
it goes beyond hope

as i get older
i have seen the world
can't begin to tell you
how i chose my path
seems god had a plan

there have been many days
with full of surprises
take this time together
laugh, cry, and remember

be grateful for kind friends
the laughter and the tears
enjoyed all the experiences
hugs and kisses with family's touch

god gave me an opportunity
renewal of my mind
restore to freshness
compassion and knowledge
make spiritually new
rebirth and renew
an extraordinary life

god gave me a chance
a family i newly found
from being a lonely child
to three loving sisters
many stir emotions

discovered our deeper bonds

from being feeling lonely
to a full family with love
sisters in my life
it's the most wonderful thing

my prayers had answered
thank god for three sisters
from now everyday
i drew closer to god

sisters are my blessings
memories will last forever

long lost sister found

i had no sister since little
to call when i was in distress
i'd never experienced
having sisters in my life
can be a wonderful feeling

decided to find my family
did the DNA testing
twenty years passed by
long lost family found

i have three sisters now
who can give me advice
their comforting words
worth much more than dimes

still think it was a dream
had to pinch myself
laughed and cried in a mixed
no one can comprehend my thoughts

having a sister is not just a trend
i not just have one
but three altogether
hopes and dreams yet reached

now it's time for me to say
what you mean to me
is more than i can express
i love you
is that too much to say

i don't think you could ever know
just how special you are
i don't think you could ever feel
all the love i have to give

he was making us for each other
to share life's smiles and tears
i never could have imagined
what a sister's love was about
until i met you, i really found
a sister's love is unconditional
a love that has no end
a sister's love is the best
a love that always defends

be grateful for the morning dew
the grass beneath our feet
the tenderness of kindly hearts
shared our days of gloom

sometimes i may think i'm alone
think of having you in my life
completes and fulfills every part of me

i am thankful

a woman
with the heart of gold
a woman
with the love like a saint

i am thankful
thankful for your heart of gold
i am thankful
thankful for your love like a saint

when i was young
you were my strength
you were my angel
the giver of life

your loving touch
ready for the day ahead
never gave up
on my hopes, and dreams
you always said
faith brought me to you

i am thankful
your tenderness of kindly hearts
without you

how can I survive
without you
what I have become

a woman
with the heart of gold
a stranger
who i called mother

a mother
sacrifice everything for me
a woman
with the love like a saint

a stranger
who i called mother
a mother
i indebtedness for life
i am thankful
thankful for your heart of gold
i am thankful
thankful for your love like a
saint

i am thankful
but most of all
i'm thankful for you

i am proud

as the leftover of the unpopular
war
a motherland, where i was born
into
straddling two worlds but
belonging to neither
i was put up for adoption since
birth

growing up in Vietnam
life wasn't easy
faith took me through the most challenging
times
but i am proud to be a
Vietnamese
while much of hope lived in the
mind
once shunned by many
sustained by a single dream

a fatherland, that gave me an
open door
i am proud to be an american
from this new place of freedom
it was an incredible feeling

each new day presents a new
future
on the new road, i become a new
person

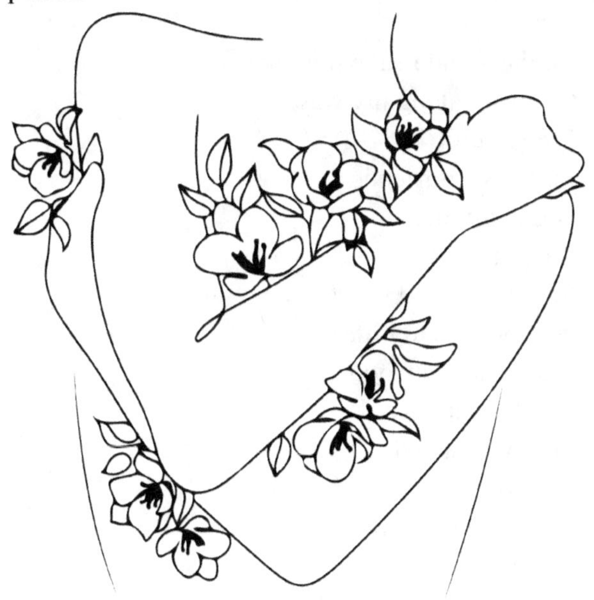

be grateful

i'm grateful
for the wonderful children
that walk along my way
i'm grateful
for the kind friends
you in my life
i'm grateful
for my beloved mom
you touched my life
and made me who i am
i'm grateful
for my husband
you are
an amazing person
without you
i don't know where i'd be
be grateful
for the health you own
the work you find to do
for round about you
there are others less fortunate than you

my little girl

twenty years ago
from today's date
my contractions started
strong cramping
in the abdomen
groin, back with the achy feelings
twenty years ago
from today's date
my husband fell
hit his head
fainted over my epidural injection

mom was in pain
dad was out cold
grandma was confused
with all the locomotions
our main focus was
waiting for you
come to see our world

November twentieth
full emotions of joy
with fear and painful
over the nine months
today is your day

to see the world
with you we born
i heard your cry
i knew it right then
you are the treasure of my life

from the moment i found
i am having you
life's been radically changed
nothing is better than
watching you grow
tiny little feet
to dancing feet
my little girl
who is not little anymore
my little girl
now grown into a fine young woman
you have turned out
such an intelligent
fun and caring person

my lovely daughter
on your birthday
the day you celebrate
come once a year
for twenty years
i am reminded
how thankful I am
how joyful I am

with many hugs
kisses and love
happy birthday to beautiful you
my little girl

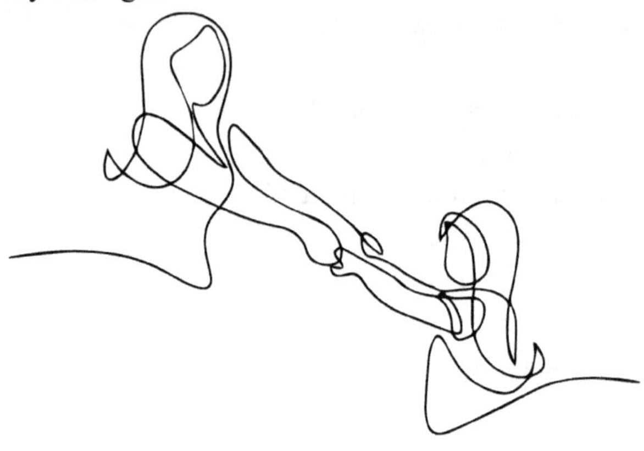

fly high

never thought of having kid
into this world you came
on a cool breezing day
i pondered, and i thought
you'll never fully understand

i never liked to have a kid
so annoying i thought
as i get older
my life and the time
had moved by so fast

for this i don't complain
for this i'm not ashamed
i realize throughout many years
i've been through it all
time had made me change

once you entered my life
and you are my girl
forever in my heart
i am happy though
my girl is an angel

also, a companion to whom

i can express my feelings to
you are my best friend
we share a common theme
which reminds me of the past

i left the house at eighteen
a gentleman had told me
you can die on the street
never to come back here
and i promised to myself
never turned to look back

never regretted my choice
knowing the path that i chose
rough and curvy roads i experienced them all

now, it's your turn my dear
you have wings to fly
though you might ill-equipped
but life will show you how,
to navigate your way through

be grateful for the growing trees
the roses soon to bloom
the birds soon to fly
you choose your own path

although we've had our separate lives
whether you have ups or downs

i always help you dear
never with a frown

whether we're near or far apart
we'll always be close
although we've had our separate lives
never forget,
i am always here

when you are not around
my days are full of strife
i was stubborn at your age
you reminded me my days
difficult areas of growing up

that is the way of life
now you left your nest
emptiness i feel
when you're by my side
my world is filled with life
all our laughter sweet
you're my brightest star

flap your wings to the sky
fly high with big dreams
you rise like a star
with the beauty of a dove
as sweet as milk chocolate

flap your wings to the sky
fly high with big dreams
full of joy like a rainbow
everything is smooth as fudge
you will make mama proud
i love you Victoria
i dedicate this poem to you

blessings sent from heaven

there were moments in my life
i thought i'm done with you
so we can go our separate ways
you were never here for me
while I'm sinking with sorrow and fear
you said you love me
but all you care is work
never had time for me

there were moments in my life
divorce goes churning through my mind
i wondered aloud to my kids
i'd never fully understand
conflicts stop me in my tracks
there were moments in my life
you cheated on me
my heart bled and hurt
feeling betrayed and so lost
my heart is left abate
i crumbled and fell apart

questioning whether or not
the marriage should be ended
I asked god for the light
to get my mind straight

and open my heavy heart
he asked me do two things
first,
looked within your heart
you will find the answers
second,
look for the good
instead of the bad

instead tried to salvage
we both worked it out
the marriage continued
maybe even for life

being hurt by the one you love
although it is hard at first

you have changed in so many ways
you're more thoughtful and considerate
a much happier outcome
you've came to open my heart
you tell me every day
you love me on my bad days
you've been my will to live
how much you mean to me
for all the todays and tomorrows
i'm grateful for all that i have
the blessings sent from heaven above

enjoy the autumn fall

life is like the season
always change and unpredictable
we have summer, spring
and autumn then winter
from sunshine, rain to cold
similar life
it's own phase
from sadness to happiness

our life
it's own phase
just like seasons change
small changes
how we cope
getting into a new habit
being appreciative of all things
letting go of the past
celebrating with the new
that makes me so happy
the summer now is gone
welcome autumn is here
green leaves start changing

autumn known as fall
as days grow shorter
and nights grow longer

as the season begins
cooler crisp autumn fall
trees start to light up
reds, oranges, and gold
autumn colors in parks
in cities and countryside
takes a scenic drive
anywhere you may find

celebrate autumn color fest
sip on local brew
dance to live music
gathering friends for feast
get into the fresh start
reconnect and celebrate
enjoy the autumn fall

thanksgiving

what is thanksgiving
may i ask
thanksgiving
is a holiday
to celebrate the harvest
blessings of the year
it's a holiday
everywhere in the world
not just exclude america
in asia or Vietnam, too
it's the time
for families to celebrate

thanksgiving
we call moon fest
it's when the moon
is at its fullest
to pray for the harvest
all the things we have
It's also called
autumn fest
to pray for fine weather
peace for the country

thanksgiving
oh, how we love

family gatherings
the foods we eat
in america
the favorite food
it's roast turkey
in Vietnam
the favorite food
moon cake, it is
here in america
i can have
two holidays
moon fest and thanksgiving
we can eat two favorite foods

thank you much
for all that i have
family
friends
dogs
and my favorite food
my stuffed roasted turkey
thanksgiving
oh, how I love
family gatherings
with my favorite foods

wishing everyone
a happy thanksgiving

holiday grief

it's been ten years now
i lost someone dear to me
the pain of loss was subsided
every morning i wake up
i just have to push
myself out of bed
to keep going forward
fighting and surviving
find a reason to live
a reason to keep persevering
motivation on display
inspirational poem to keep

every year is the same
it's the hardest time
these months of the year
can reopen the wounds
when holidays come
we remember to celebrate shared with our loved
ones
who are no longer with us

grief is a natural response
it's the emotional pain
we do need healing

during this part of the year much more than we
need presents or parties

holiday causes us to feel
the world around us
with greater awareness
it's also an excellent time
to mend our past pains
and gain a new
more positive perspective

we can evolve through
this time of the year
by healing our minds
body and spirits

Conclusion

there is always hope in life
even when we're down
or life smacks us around
mind, body and spirit
breath, smile and survive
love and all the merit
stand strong to conquer all

Thank You

I am thankful and grateful to have you on my journey. Your support means a lot to me.

toanh.nguyen1481 - Instagram
Nguyễn TốAnh - Facebook
Customer Care Representative - Mechanics Bank
toanh09@hotmail.com

Tree Franklyn—Bestselling Author, Founder of the Empathic Awakening Academy. She helps people master their energy so they can heal their past and create a new and empowered future.
https://treefranklyn.com